Uzaki-chan Wants to Hang Out!
3
story & art
Take
D0992838

CONTENTS

Chapter 24: The Kouhai and Kouhai's House

YOU'RE SO THOUGHTFUL, SENPAI-- WANTING TO PAY US BACK AND ALL.
MY MOM SAID IT'S FINE, YOU KNOW.
SUGOI DEKAI
NAW, YOU GAVE ME TOO MUCH.
AND SINCE YOU WON'T TAKE THE MONEY...
I HAVE TO RETURN IT TO HER.
IT'S ONLY "TOO MUCH" 'CAUSE YOU BOUGHT A CHEAP FUTON, RIGHT?
YOU SHOULDA TAKEN THE OPPORTUNITY TO BUY A *NICE* ONE.
SUGOI DEKAI
?
......

YOU'RE KINDA QUIET TODAY.
TWITCH

NER-VOUS?
OHH...
IS THIS YOUR FIRST TIME GOING TO A GIRL'S HOUSE?
SUGOI DEKAI

YEAH.
I HAVE THIS KINDA HEAVINESS IN MY STOMACH...
YOU GET WEAK UNDER PRES-SURE, HUH?

WHAT DO YOU THINK MY PLACE IS?
A HAUNTED HOUSE OR SOME-THING?
I WON'T BITE.
U-UH-HUH...

ANYWAY, I'VE GOT CATS YOU CAN PET ALL YOU LIKE.
TWITCH
PWAAA
THAT WAS A QUICK TURN-AROUND.
YOU REALLY LIKE CATS *THAT* MUCH BETTER THAN ME?
THAT'S KINDA IRRITATING!
KA-CHAK
LOOK, WE'RE HERE.
I TOLD MY MOM I WAS BRING-ING YOU OVER.
I'M HOOO-ME!
SHF パタ
SHF パタ
WELCOME HOME!

OH, HELLO!
ARE YOU HANA'S SENPAI?
Uzaki Tsuki (43)

LOO OOM
I'VE HEARD SO MUCH ABOUT YOU FROM HANA...

SCARY.

H-HIS GLARE IS LIKE DAGGERS... THIS IS NO ORDINARY BOY...
SHE DIDN'T EVEN TELL ME HE WAS A BOY!
HE'S BIG... SO SCARY...
TWITCH TWITCH
H-HELLO, I'M HANA'S MOTHER...
FIDGET オド
FIDGET オド
GOOD TO MEET YOU. I'M SAKURAI.
BOW
THANK YOU FOR PAYING FOR MY FUTON.
MY... MUCH POLITER THAN HE LOOKS.
BUT YOU OVERPAID, SO I'D LIKE TO RETURN THE EXTRA...
His face is stiff because he's nervous.
YEEP...!
ギヌロ
DEATH GLARE
AH, I CAN'T! HIS EYES ARE JUST SO SCARY!!
HEY, SEN-PAI...
DON'T STAND IN THE DOORWAY AND TALK. COME ON IN.
UH, BUT... I WAS GOING TO GO STRAIGHT HOME AFTER RETURNING THE MONEY...
HUH?! HE'S COMING IN?
THAT'S RIGHT, YOU CAN'T KEEP HIM HERE, HANA!

WELL THEN...
IF YOU INSIST...
SHWOOOOM
YEEEEEP...!
Shiishika ♂
Nika ♀
I SEE...

SO, I GAVE YOU TOO MUCH FOR THAT FUTON HANA RUINED, AND YOU CAME TO RETURN THE LEFTOVER MONEY...
YEAH.
SO FAR AWAY...
SO FAR AWAY...
I TRIED GIVING IT TO HANA-SAN...
BUT SHE WOULDN'T TAKE IT, SO I CAME HERE. SORRY TO BOTHER YOU.
HUH? I SAID THAT ALREADY, DIDN'T I?
FIDGET
I UNDER-STAND. COULD YOU WAIT A MO-MENT?
HANA.
COME HERE.
HM? WHAT IS IT?
YOU ONLY TOLD ME THIS WAS "A SENPAI FROM SCHOOL"...
YOU NEVER MEN-TIONED YOU STAYED OVER AT A BOY'S HOUSE!
STREEETCH
OW OW OW OW OW OW!
YEAH, THAT'LL GET YOUR PARENTS MAD.

BUT SENPAI'S OKAY...
STREEEETCH
THAT'S NOT THE POINT!
HE'S STILL, UM... YOU KNOW!
I CAN'T SAY ANYTHING...
I DID SUSPECT THIS, A LITTLE...
HAAH...
I'M SORRY FOR ALL THE TROUBLE MY DAUGHTER HAS CAUSED YOU.
OH NO, NOT AT ALL...
NO, NO...
FEEL FREE TO SCOLD HER MORE, THOUGH.
THIS IS A GOOD OPPORTUNITY, AFTER ALL.
DEADPAN...
SENPAI ?!

SENPAI?! YOU THINK MY ATTENTION IS A BOTHER?!
HA HA HA!
OH, NOT AT ALL.
I'M THANKFUL FOR IT MAYBE ONE OUT OF TEN TIMES.
MY BATTING AVERAGE IS .10?!
YOU TURKEY!!
I'M STARTING TO UNDERSTAND YOUR DYNAMIC...
HANA DOES ALWAYS COME HOME SAFELY, THOUGH.
AND SHE ENJOYS GOING TO SCHOOL.
HRM...
ANYWAY, THEY SEEM TO GET ALONG.
THIS MAN IS A GOOD SENPAI AND A GOOD FRIEND.
HE LOOKS SCARY AT FIRST, BUT HE SEEMS EARNEST, WHICH IS A RELIEF...
TROT
TROT
I WAS WORRYING TOO MUCH.
STILL, FOR HANA TO BRING A BOY OVER...
I MIGHT HAVE SOMETHING ELSE TO WORRY ABOUT IN THE FUTURE...
TEE HEE...

WAIT-- HIS GAZE IS A LITTLE LOWER.

IT'S AIMED AT MY...

GASP!

CHEST?!

WANNA TOUCH, SENPAI? (MEANING THE CAT.)
HANA ?!
SUGOI DEKAI
WELL, IF I COULD... (MEANING THE CAT.)
SAKU-RAI-KUN?!
YOU PROBABLY CAN'T YET. SHE LOOKS SKITTISH-- I DON'T THINK SHE'LL COME CLOSE JUST YET.
COME CLOSE ?!
YET ?!
'CAUSE SHE'S SHY.
THIS ISN'T ABOUT SHY-NESS!!
FWP
FWP
IF YOU STOP BY OFTEN AND SHE GETS USED TO YOU, SHE MIGHT COME FOR YOU SOME-DAY!
NEVER! NO WAY!
HOW CAN YOU SAY SUCH THINGS IN FRONT OF YOUR MOTH-ER?!
YEAH...
EVEN IF IT WON'T HAPPEN NOW...
I'D LIKE TO TOUCH THAT PUSSY SOME-DAY.

THANKS.
HUH?!
I'LL GET GOING NOW.
SINCE I'VE RETURNED THE MONEY.
AH...!
U-UM...
YOU'RE GOING HOME? LET'S PLAY GAMES IN MY ROOM!
NAW, I DON'T WANT TO OVER-STAY MY WEL-COME.
CAN I COME TO YOUR PLACE THEN, SENPAI? LET'S HANG OUT!
IF YOU WANT, I GUESS...
SUGOI DEKAI
THANKS FOR HAVING ME.
SEE YOU.
I'M HEAD-ING OUT, MOM!
BA-TNK
KLATTA
KLATTA
WHY...
WHY IS MY HEART...
RACING LIKE THIS?
DMP
DMP
DMP
DMP
He's activated a weird kink.

SHE USED TO BE REALLY INTO SOME INTENSE SOAP OPERAS.

Uzaki-chan Wants to Hang Out!

I'M GONNA GO WORK NOW! TAKE IT EASY, 'KAY?
WORK HARD!

SO HE WORKS AT THE SAME CAFÉ AS HANA-CHAN, HUH?

I CAME TO CHECK IT OUT...

BUT SHE DIDN'T TELL ME SAKURAI-KUN WOULD BE HERE, TOO!
BA-DMP
BA-DMP
TWITCH
TWITCH

Chapter 25: The Kouhai and Her Mom

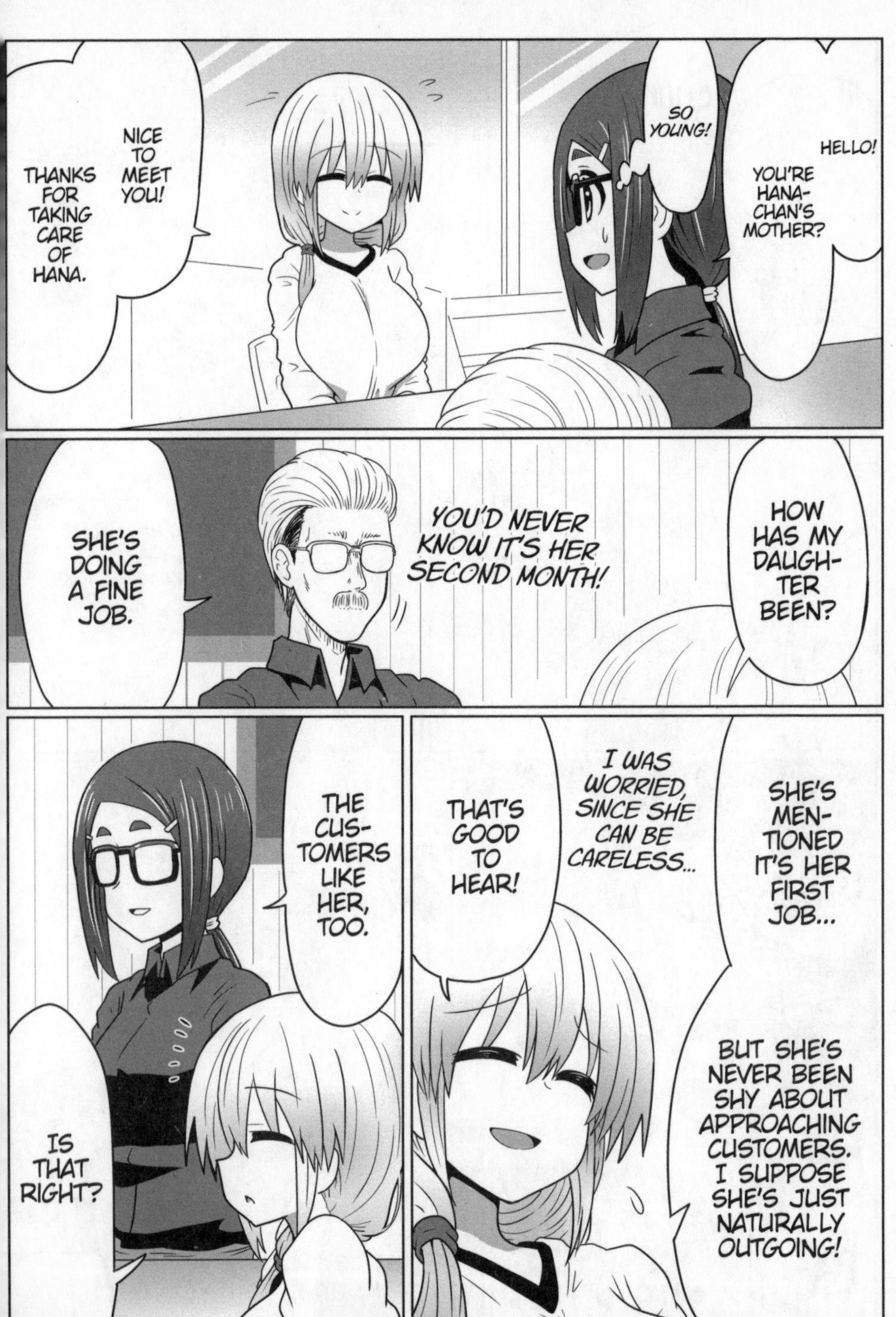
HELLO! YOU'RE HANA-CHAN'S MOTHER?
SO YOUNG!
NICE TO MEET YOU!
THANKS FOR TAKING CARE OF HANA.
HOW HAS MY DAUGHTER BEEN?
YOU'D NEVER KNOW IT'S HER SECOND MONTH!
SHE'S DOING A FINE JOB.
SHE'S MENTIONED IT'S HER FIRST JOB...
I WAS WORRIED, SINCE SHE CAN BE CARELESS...
THAT'S GOOD TO HEAR!
BUT SHE'S NEVER BEEN SHY ABOUT APPROACHING CUSTOMERS. I SUPPOSE SHE'S JUST NATURALLY OUTGOING!
THE CUSTOMERS LIKE HER, TOO.
IS THAT RIGHT?

CHECK OUT THAT TABLE. IT'S A GROUP ON THEIR WAY BACK FROM KINDER-GARTEN.
THIS AREA'S RESIDENTIAL, SO MOST OF THE CUSTOMERS ARE HOUSEWIVES, WHO OFTEN BRING THEIR KIDS.
SULK—
THE KIDS GET BORED WHEN THE MOMS START CHAT-TING...
BUT HANA-CHAN GIVES THEM ATTEN-TION...
WELCOME!
WHEN-EVER SHE GETS A FREE MOMENT.
HUNH
...
SO SHE'S POPULAR WITH THE KIDS!

SHE KEEPS THEM BUSY, SO THE MOMS CAN CHAT IN PEACE.
LET'S GO PLAY OVER THERE!
I SEE...
I WAS WOR-RIED ABOUT HER...
BUT NOW I FEEL A LITTLE RE-LIEVED!
I'M A PARENT TOO, SO I KNOW WHAT YOU MEAN.
CUSTOM-ERS COME IN WITH VARIOUS GOALS.
THESE FLYERS ARE BLANK ON THE BACK.
MAYBE IT'S TO CHECK OUT THE CAFÉ, OR BE SERVED, OR JUST TO EAT AND DRINK...
MOST FIRST-TIME EMPLOYEES DON'T PICK UP ON THOSE GOALS AND ACT ON THEM.
SHE HAS, THOUGH.

MINDING CHILDREN ISN'T SUPPOSED TO BE A SERVER'S JOB...
AND I'M SURE THE CUSTOMERS NEVER CAME EXPECTING IT.
HANA-CHAN'S REALLY GOING ABOVE AND BEYOND THE CALL OF DUTY!
AND SHE JUST DOES THAT NATURALLY.
IDEAL CUSTOMER SERVICE IS MAKING YOUR CUSTOMERS YOUR FANS.
AFTER ALL, IF THEY'RE FANS, THEY'LL COME AROUND MORE OFTEN.
BEING THE REASON THEY KEEP COMING IN IS A BIG STRENGTH.
SUCH WORDS MAKE A MOTHER PROUD.
I'M GLAD SHE'S BEING USEFUL.

THOSE MOMS DO HAVE ONE PARTICULAR AIM, HOWEVER...
YOU MEAN... SAKURAI-KUN?
YOU KNOW HIM?
A LITTLE ...
AS I SAID, HOUSEWIVES ARE OUR GREATEST CUSTOMER BASE...
AND HE'S INCREDIBLY POPULAR WITH THEM.
?!
HUP!
HE TENDS TO LOOK A LITTLE GRUMPY, BUT ONCE YOU GET USED TO HIM, YOU NOTICE HIS FACE IS RATHER HANDSOME, AND THAT HE'S TALL, SLENDER, AND MUSCULAR.
ALSO EARNEST AND POLITE, WHICH MAKES HIM A RATHER NICE CATCH.
NOW THAT YOU MENTION IT... MAYBE YOU'RE RIGHT...

HE GREW UP ON SPORTS TEAMS, SO HE SPEAKS TO HIS ELDERS WITH RESPECT. MOST OF ALL, HE HAS CONFI-DENCE.
I THINK THAT'S THE TYPE ADULTS LIKE.
IT'S RE-FRESHING, TALKING TO HIM.
I SEE...
SOMEONE WATCHES THEIR KIDS AND THEY GET TO CHAT WITH A YOUNG STUD--OF COURSE THE MOMS ARE GONNA BE FANS.
WE'RE DOING GOOD BUSI-NESS!
HEH HEH HEH HEH...
STOP TALKING ABOUT YOUR DAD'S BUSINESS IN SUCH DUBIOUS TERMS!
THIS ISN'T SOME KIND OF SCHEME. THE KIDS WANT TO GO OFF WITH HER!
I GET WHY HE'S GAINED FANS...
BUT I WON-DER...
WHAT ABOUT HIM ...?
??

WHAT DO YOU MEAN?
AH! UM, ER-- HOW SHOULD I PUT IT...
I WONDER...
IF MARRIED WOMEN...
MUTTER...
OR OLDER WOMEN... ARE HIS TYPE...
OH... SHE...
THIS FATHER-DAUGHTER TEAM HAVE SERVED CUSTOMERS FOR MANY YEARS. THEY'VE SEEN IT ALL. THEY UNDERSTAND HUMAN NATURE.
BOSS.
BA-DMP

I'M CARRYING IN THE BEANS, SO I'LL ORGANIZE THE STORE-ROOM WHILE I'M AT IT.
HAAH
IT SEEMS... THERE'S BEEN A MISUNDER-STAND-ING...
MA'AM, IT'S ALL RIGHT. HE'S NO COUGAR-KILLER.
HE'S JUST RATHER DENSE.
IS...
IS THAT RIGHT?
HE'S QUITE EASILY MISUN-DER-STOOD...
PLEASE, DON'T WORRY.
HE AND YOUR DAUGH-TER GET ALONG WELL AND ENJOY THE WORK.
NOT A MAR-RIED WO-MAN!
NOT A MAR-RIED WO-MAN!
THEY BOTH READ BETWEEN THE LINES.

SILLY ME... WHAT WAS I THINKING!
HOW EMBARRASSING! PLEASE FORGET ABOUT IT...
JUST LIKE HER DAUGHTER WHEN SHE'S EMBARRASSED...
ANYWAY...
AHEM...
I'M RELIEVED TO SEE MY DAUGHTER'S BEEN WORKING IN SUCH A NICE PLACE.
SHE HAS HER FLAWS...
BUT I HOPE YOU WILL TAKE CARE OF HER.
THANK YOU VERY MUCH FOR TODAY.
OH, NO-- THANK YOU.
I HAVE TO HEAD OUT NOW...
I'LL JUST LET HANA KNOW BEFORE I LEAVE.
ゴソ RSTL
ゴソ RSTL
SENPAAAAI?
DO YOU NEED HELP?
ゴソ RSTL

DON'T WORRY ABOUT IT.
THERE'S A LOT, PLUS THEY'RE PRETTY HEAVY.
SO IT'LL BE HARD HANDLING IT ALL ALONE, RIGHT?
TUG
グイッ
AH ...!
DON'T LIFT THAT BY THE CORNER!
HUH?
RRRIP
FSHH
AHH!
UWAAH! COFFEE BEANS!
DO I HAVE TO PAY FOR THIS?!
IS NOW REALLY THE TIME TO ASK ME THAT?!
SKATA
SKATA
SKATA
SKATA
SKATA
SKATA
SKATA
WAAAH! I-I HAVE TO PLUG UP THE HOLE!
COVER IT WITH YOUR HANDS FIRST!
HANA, I HAVE TO GO NOW...

ACK! SENPAI, IT'S COMING OUT HERE, TOO!!

IT'S ALL SPILLING, AHH!

DON'T MOVE, IT'LL SPILL EVEN MORE!!

WAGH! WHAT DO I DO?!

Staff Only

I'VE NEVER SEEN THIS STUFF BEFORE. IT'S SUCH A CLOUDY OFF-WHITE, HUH?

WHAT DO YOU DO? ONCE YOU SPRAY OUT SUCH A BIG LOAD, THERE'S NOTHING YOU CAN DO...

WE JUST HAVE TO CLEAN UP...

WMP

SLUMP...

SORRY...

BUT COULD YOU CALL ME A TAXI...?

SLUMP...

STAGGER...

THOSE KIDS... I KNEW IT...

?!

THE MISUNDER-STAND-INGS DEEP-ENED.

Black sleeveless undershirt.

Uzaki-chan Wants to Hang Out!

Chapter 26: The Kouhai and a Gaffe

I'LL DO WHATEVER IT TAKES TO GET YOUR GOAT, SENPAI!
GLINT
IS THAT REALLY SOME-THING TO GLOAT ABOUT...
CHEAT-ER?
THAT'S WHAT THEY CALL THE HOWL OF THE LOSING DOG, SENPAI.
HA HA, LOSER!
PFFT!
PFFT! HEE HEE!
LOSER DOG!
IRK
LOSER DOG
I'M GONNA GET A DRINK...
GET ONE FOR ME, TOO!
UH, WHY ...?
HUH?
YOU LOST--YOU SHOULD AT LEAST RUN ONE ERRAND FOR ME, RIGHT?
FINE... WHAT-EVER.

OHH, MAYBE WE SHOULD'VE BET SOME-THING ON IT.
LIKE THAT PRICEY NEW PUD-DING.
YOU COULD RUN TO THE CORNER STORE FOR IT.
YOU'RE GETTING PRETTY FULL OF YOUR-SELF.
WHY CAN'T YOU BE GENTLE AND KIND LIKE YOUR MOM?
GRUMBLE
ブツクサ
GRUMBLE
ブツクサ
MIFFED
THE NEXT DAY.
CHECK, PLEASE.

BEAM
THANK YOU SO VERY MUCH~!
PLEASE COME AGAIN SOON!

UZAKI-CHAN... IS SOMETHING WRONG...?
TEE HEE HEE HEE!
Regulars.

THANX, GUYZ!
DON'T BE SO CASUAL!!
USUALLY, SHE'S LIKE...

SHWP
SHWP

FLICK
YOU DID SOME-THING, DIDN'T YOU?
FLICK
FLICK
FLICK
FLICK
FLICK
THAT'S COLD!
FINE, YEAH-- I DID SOME-THING!
STOP FLICKING ME!
ONE CAT-CHAT LATER, MEOW...
I SEE..
OF COURSE THAT'D MAKE HER MAD.
YOU'RE SO IN-SENSI-TIVE.
HRMM...
POLITE-NESS IS ALL WELL AND GOOD...
BUT THIS IS DISTURBING THE REGULARS. SO WHAT DO WE DO?
うぐっ... NGH...

I'VE FINISHED TIDYING THINGS UP~!
OH, DEAR ME!
TEE HEE!
IT'S NOT PROPER TO BE IDLY CONVERSING JUST BECAUSE THERE ARE NO CUSTOMERS!
SHIVER
WHAT-EVER IS THE MATTER, SENPAI?
YOU'RE GAZING AT ME SO ODDLY!
SMILE...
STOP IT...
STOP WHAT~?
TALKING LIKE THAT. I KINDA DON'T LIKE IT.
AND THOSE GES-TURES.
RUB RUB

O MY
YESTERDAY YOU WISHED FOR ME TO BE MORE POLITE; TODAY, YOU'D HAVE ME STOP~?
TEE HEE HEE!
WHAT-EVER WILL I DO WITH YOU, SENPAI~?
AGHHH!
STOP IT! I JUST... JUST... REALLY HATE IT!
STOP GOING "TEE HEE"!!
ARE YOU QUIT ALL RIGHT SENPA
IF YOU'RE FEELING UNWELL, WHY DON'T YOU TAKE A LITTLE REST?
I CAN HANDLE YOUR WORK AS WELL AS MY OWN.
PLEASE, MIND YOUR HEALTH!
STO-OO-OP!
WHY DOES HER BEING NICE BOTHER YOU SO MUCH?

PLEASE DON'T PUSH YOURSELF!
IF ANYTHING WERE TO HAPPEN TO YOU, I--
STOP PLAYING "GOOD KOUHAI," YOU HUGE-ASS FAKER!
DON'T GIMME THAT BULLSHIT!!
GIVE ME THE USUAL BULLSHIT, LIKE USUAL!!
CALM DOWN, SAKURAI-KUN.
YOU'RE STARTING TO LOSE YOUR WORDS.
SAKURAI-KUN...
I THINK THIS IS CUTE TOO, IN ITS OWN WAY.
IN FACT, A CERTAIN KIND OF CUSTOMER--
AMI, BACK OFF FOR A BIT.

HMM...
SMIRK
SMIRK
IF YOU HATE IT SO MUCH, I COULD STOP.
BUT FIRST ...
YOU HAVE SOME-THING TO SAY TO ME, DON'T YOU, SENPAI?
ジトー...
STARE...
...
...

I WAS WRONG...
I'M SORRY.

COMPLETE VICTORY
SMIRK...
WE UNDERSTAND EACH OTHER, THEN.

BIG, SCARY-FACED SAKURAI-KUN MEEKLY APOLOGIZING...
ANOTHER POSSIBLE SERVICE FOR THE HOUSEWIFE SECTOR...
AMI, BE QUIET A BIT.

I LIKE HOW YOU NORMALLY ARE.

AHH, THERE IT IS ...!
SAKURAI-KUN DOING THE USUAL!! (THE THOUGHT-LESS SINCERITY ATTACK!!)

IT'S WORK-ING, IT'S WORK-ING!

SERIOUSLY-- WHEN YOU'RE LIKE THAT, SENPAI...
HUH? THERE STILL A PROBLEM?
FWP

...!!
WHAT?! I DON'T WANNA HEAR THAT FROM YOU!!

YEAH! YOU'RE ALWAYS SAYING THINGS LIKE THAT WITHOUT A THOUGHT IN YOUR HEAD!!

HOW ABOUT WE HAVE THEM CHANGE THEIR PERSONALITIES MONDAYS, WEDNESDAYS, AND FRIDAYS-- JUST FOR CUSTOMER SERVICE PURPOSES?

THE LADIES WOULD *LOVE* "MEEK SAKURAI-KUN."

I DON'T THINK THIS WOULD BE A CAFÉ ANYMORE IF WE DID THAT.

IT'D BE... SOME OTHER KIND OF ESTABLISHMENT.

GRAH GRAH GRAH GRAH

IF I DON'T WATCH OUT, I'M GONNA START GRINNING ALL OVER THE PLACE...
ぐに MUSH
ぐに MUSH
?
むに SMUSH
むに SMUSH

Uzaki-chan Wants to Hang Out!

You at home today, Senpai?
Can I come over now?
......
Sure, I guess ...
......
Right, I'm on my way!
Sakurai Shinichi was in a bad mood.
Uzaki just keeps coming over, day after day...
Well, whatever.
I give up.
At least she's started warning me first.
But...
TAP
TAP
The reason for his bad mood...

WAS THE STATE OF HIS APARTMENT.
ごちゃあ...
CLUTTER...
SHE NEVER TAKES HER STUFF HOME.

Chapter 27:
The Kouhai and Senpai's Apartment

I DIDN'T EVEN NOTICE IT, BUT NOW THERE'S A PILE!
GATHERED TOGETHER FOR THE MOMENT.
SHE BRINGS SOMETHING NEW EVERY TIME SHE COMES OVER.

WHY HAS A CORNER OF MY APARTMENT WOUND UP BEING HER SPACE?
IRK
IRK
HOW MANY CHARGERS DOES SHE HAVE?
I'VE GOT TO BE CLEAR WITH HER THIS TIME...

DING DONG DINDON DIIIN DOOONG
SHE'S HERE! THAT LITTLE TWERP!

COMING IIIN!
SENPAI, TODAY I BROUGHT A GIANT CUSHION!
LOOK, LOOK! IT'S SHAPED LIKE A TREE FROG!!
THAT'S WAY TOO BIG!!
GWAM
ドズゥム
MY FROOOG!
WHERE'S THIS COMING FROM, SENPAI?!
SHUT UP!
JUST SIT DOWN!
WAAAAH!
LATER MEOWN ...
UZAKI...
I NEED TO TALK TO YOU.

ARE YOU CONFESSING YOUR LOVE?!
OH NO, WHAT DO I DO?
N-NO!
IT'S NOT THAT!

IT'S ABOUT POSSESSIONS.

POSSESSIONS? YOU MEAN LIKE, GHOST-WISE?
WOOO...
THAT'S NOT WHAT I MEAN EITHER!
SHIVER
IT'S OKAY. THE ONE BEHIND YOU IS JUST PASSING BY.
SERIOUSLY, ENOUGH NONSENSE!

YOU NEVER TAKE YOUR STUFF BACK HOME, AND IT'S CLUTTERING UP MY APARTMENT!
YOU CAN DO IT BIT BY BIT--BUT JUST TAKE SOMETHING BACK TODAY!

SO CUTE!
THAT'S WHAT I WAS GONNA SAY, BUT THEN YOU BROUGHT THAT HUGE THING OVER.
IT'S BIGGER THAN *YOU!!*
BUT SENPAI, IT'S SO NICE!
IT'S A TREE FROG!
I DON'T CARE!
AND IT COMES WITH ITS OWN BABY.
TUP
THAT'S... A LITTLE CUTE... *BUT!*
COME ON, SENPAI-- JUST LISTEN, 'KAY?
WE SIT ON THE FLOOR AND GAME FOR A LONG TIME, RIGHT?
IT HURTS MY BUTT. CAN YOU LIVE WITH THAT?
MGH...
YOU'RE THE HEAD OF THE HOUSE-HOLD-- SHOULDN'T YOU PRE-PARE THE LIVING SPACE TO WELCOME GUESTS?
OR ARE YOU GOING TO TAKE RESPON-SIBILITY FOR MY STIFF BUTT?
BLAH
BLAH
BLAH
BLAH
BLAH
YOU'RE SHAME-LESS...

HEY, HEY...
AND SO I PLEAD NOT GUILTY OF IMPROPER CUSHION-ING.
YOU CAN USE IT WHEN I'M NOT AROUND, TOO.
YOU'RE THE ONE BRINGING YOUR-SELF OVER ALL THE TIME.
FINE. CUSHIONS AND SITTING CUSHIONS ARE SAFE.
HAAH...
JUST MAKE SURE TO TAKE THEM BACK SOME DAY.
HOW-EVER!
THE REAL PROB-LEM IS *THAT.*
THAT PILE OF ALL THE STUFF YOU'VE LEFT HERE.
ビッ JAB
HUUUH, THERE'S QUITE A LOT, ISN'T THERE?
DON'T ACT LIKE IT'S NOT YOUR PROBLEM!
I'M GOING TO START SORTING OUT WHAT TO THROW AWAY.
I'M NOT GONNA LET YOU PLAY UNTIL IT'S DONE.
ごろり LAZE
AGH, WHAT A PAAAIN!
ボフッ BOOF
IF WE DON'T DO IT, MY APARTMENT'S GONNA KEEP SHRINK-ING!!

LET'S SORT THIS QUICKLY
EVERY-THING YOU DON'T WANT, I'M TOSSING IN GARBAGE BAGS TODAY.
ANYTHING YOU WANT, TAKE HOME.
FIIINE.
バサッ RUSTLE
HOW ABOUT THESE?
DON'T WANT 'EM.
Various discarded paper bags.
AND THESE?
NOPE.
Empty gacha capsules.
AND THESE?
NOPE.
Boring, crappy DVDs.
THIS'S JUST JUNK TO YOU!
DON'T BRING IT TO MY PLACE! JUST THROW IT OUT!!
AHHH, HA HA HA!
SOME-TIMES IT'S HARD TO KNOW IF YOU REALLY WANNA THROW SOME-THING OUT!
ALSO, I HAVE TO ASK...

WHAT'S THIS?
OH, THAT.
A LIZARD MASK?
A FRIEND OF MINE IN THE DESIGN DEPARTMENT GAVE IT TO ME.
THEN YOU DON'T NEED IT, RIGHT?
I'M THROWING IT OUT.
AHHH, WAIT! HOLD UP A MINUTE!
THIS THING'S PRETTY INTERESTING.
RIGHT HERE, YOU BLOW IN AIR.
Eye holes
WHEN YOU PUT IT ON YOUR HEAD...
AND BLOW...
FOOO
FWAP
FWAP
FWAP
FWAP
FSSSS
FOOO
FWAP
FWAP
FWAP
FWAP
FWAP
FWAP

SO?
PWAH!!
LET'S THROW IT OUT.
WHAT?! ISN'T IT FUN?!
IT'LL BE PERFECT FOR HAL-LOWEEN!
SO WHAT?!
YOU DUMPED IT HERE AND LEFT IT BECAUSE YOU DON'T WANT IT!
THAT'S TRUE.
YOU DON'T EVEN CARE!
YOU DON'T ACTU-ALLY WANT IT!
ズボ
SHUV
I DID KINDA GET CLOSURE FROM SHOWING IT TO YOU, SENPAI.
WHAT'S THAT SUP-POSED TO MEAN?!
AFTER AN HOUR OF BATTLES AND DERAIL-MENTS...

FINALLY FINISHED.
I'VE GOTTEN BACK MY OLD SPACE.
WHEW
ギュッ TUG
I'M TIIIRED.
ぐて～ SLUMP
ボスッ BWUMF
IT WAS ONLY A BIG JOB BECAUSE YOU BROUGHT ALL THAT JUNK OVER.
AH...I KNOW WHAT'S COMING...
WHY DO I HAVE TO CLEAN UP STUFF YOU BROUGHT OVER?
AND YOU KEEP BUYING PHONE CHARGERS FOR NO REASON! YOU'RE NOT THINKING ABOUT THAT, ARE YOU?
BLAH
BLAH
BLAH
BLAH
BLAH
I KNEW IT, A LECTURE...
YEUGH...
HEY, ARE YOU LISTENING?
HUFFY
WAAH... I'VE REF-LECTED ON MY ACTIONS... PLEASE, NO MORE!
WHAT DO YOU MEAN, NO MORE?

HM ...?

WHAT'S THAT BAG BEHIND YOU?

AH.

YOU DIDN'T BRING MORE STUFF OVER, DID YOU?

YOU'VE GOT TO BE KID-DING ME. WE JUST FINISHED CLEANING UP...

AH, NO-- THAT'S...

がさり RUSTLE

THIS IS...

FOOD ...

AH... HA HA HA...

I FIGURED I'D MAKE YOU DINNER TODAY. IT'S BEEN A WHILE...

AH... UM...
UH...
IF I'D KNOWN, I'D, UH...
SENPAI.
YES?
BEEF OR FISH.
WHICH DO YOU WANT FOR THE MAIN COURSE?
......
FISH.
IT'S REALLY GOOD... SORRY...
OHO HO!
I LIKE IT WHEN YOU MEEKLY APOLOGIZE, SENPAI.
HE'S KIND OF AN EASY MARK...
MUNCH MUNCH
HIS APARTMENT GOT CLEANED UP AND HIS SOUR MOOD WAS GONE...
BUT HE NEVER NOTICED UZAKI HAD GOT HIM BY THE STOMACH.

WH-WHOA...
THIS ISN'T BAD...
SHLMP...
IT'S GREAT, RIGHT?

Uzaki-chan Wants to Hang Out!

HUH
YOU'VE SPENT A YOUR TIM WORKIN HERE SIN THAT TIM WE WEN TO THE BEACH?
SHOCK
NOT THE WHOLE TIME.
WE WENT TO SEN-PAI'S HOUSE...
PLAYED GAMES...
DID A BIG CLEAN...
PLAYED MORE GAMES...
A BIG CLEAN...?
WOW ...
THAT'S PRETTY INDOOR STUFF FOR PEOPLE WHO USED TO BE IN A SPORTS CLUB...
I MEAN, IT'S HOT OUT-SIDE.
IF IT'S COOL AT NIGHT, I GO TO THE CORNER STORE.
WHAT ARE YOU GUYS, VAM-PIRES?
YOU'RE YOUNG! THIS IS UN-HEALTHY.
NOD NOD
IN MANY WAYS.
ALL RIGHT, HOW ABOUT SOME INDOOR FUN?
IN-DOOR?

BOWL-ING?
COU-PON'S GOOD FOR UP TO FOUR PEOPLE.
HOW ABOUT TOMOR-ROW?
OHH, I GET IT. IT'S INDOORS, AND IT'S THE KIND OF THING STUDENTS DO.
1 GAME FREE!
*Until August 30th
*Offer valid for groups of up to four
*One coupon per customer
AH, NO-- WE CAN'T! BOWL-ING'S NO GOOD!!
THE TRUTH IS, SENPAI'S REALLY BAD AT BOWLING!
I MEAN, HE'S HILARIOUS! HE'LL JUST FLING THAT BALL, Y'KNOW?! KONK!
BOWLING REQUIRES PRECI-SION, AND THAT'S JUST NOT HIS THING!
BUT HE'S SLOW ABOUT LOTS OF THINGS, YOU KNOW! NO HELP FOR IT!
SO YOU'RE GOING?
PFFFT!!
YES, PLEASE.

THE NEXT DAY...
GA-KNK
GNNN
GNNN

Chapter 28: The Kouhai and Bowling

SO YEAH, IT'S BEEN A LONG TIME SINCE WE WENT BOWLING.
I THINK IT WAS ABOUT THIS TIME LAST YEAR.
SUGOI DEKAI
YOU WENT TOGETHER THEN?
YEP.
SRY! ♡
Asai-san is working today.

WATCH FOR SENPAI'S MOVES, SAKAKI-SAN.
YOU'LL GET A REAL LAUGH.
ARE YOU THAT BAD?
JUST LET HER TALK.

THANK YOU FOR WAITING. YOU CAN TAKE LANE TWELVE ON THE UPPER FLOOR.
BEEP
BEEP
THANKS.

WANNA MAKE A BET?
LIKE, THE WORST SCORER HAS TO BUY LUNCH?
I'M GOOD.
YOU TWO CAN PLAY GAMES LIKE THAT WITH-OUT ME.
SUGOI DEKAI
TWELVE, TWELVE...
HERE IT IS.
I GET FIRST THROW!
DON'T HOLD A GRUDGE IF YOU LOSE, SENPAI!
I WONDER WHAT I'LL HAVE YOU DO ONCE I WIN?
SAY WHAT YOU WANT.
YEAH, YEAH.
SWIF
SWIF
YOU'RE PRETTY CHILL TODAY, SAKU.
TRYING TO RILE ME UP IS HER STRATEGY.
IF NOT HER OBSES-SION.

I SEE. THIS MATCH...
HMM...
IS ABOUT WHETHER OR NOT YOU CAN KEEP YOUR COOL.
WHAT SORT OF GAMES DO YOU GUYS USUALLY PLAY?
I MEAN, IF OFF-THE-BOARD TACTICS ARE THE NORM...
YEAH, BUT LATELY...
はあ あ あ あ あ... HAAAAH...
I'VE JUST BEEN FEELING NUMB TO IT.
IF I FREAK OUT, I'M JUST PLAYING INTO HER HANDS.
ALL I HAVE TO DO IS IGNORE HER...
WHA...
Hana
Brat
Hottie
UZAKI! HEY !!
THE BATTLE HAS ALREADY BEGUN...

GA-KOON
AHH! I LEFT TWO!
THAT'S NOR-MAL.
THOUGH YOU WERE ACTING PRETTY CONFIDENT.
SHE DOESN'T DOMINATE ME AS MUCH AS SHE LIKES TO CLAIM.
C'MON, C'MON-- YOU'RE UP NEXT, SENPAI!!
SHUT UP!!
SUGOI DEKAI
LET'S GO, LET'S GO!
YEAH, YEAH.
YOU'VE BEEN ACTING COOL TODAY, SENPAI...
BUT YOU'LL DROP THE PRETENSE SOON ENOUGH.
Psych, psych!

BA-
KRSS
OOH, A STRIKE.
I'M NEXT.
...!!
I'M NOT PRE-TENDING.
I PRAC-TICED BY MYSELF SOME BUT DIDN'T REALLY IMPROVE.
AH!
THAT, JUST NOW...

WAS ME TAKING ALL THE ANGER YOU'VE RILED UP--AND PUTTING IT INTO THE BALL!!
DUUN
NOT COOL!!

SO YOU'VE BUILT ON YOUR HABIT OF JUST FLINGING THE BALL.
IF YOU THROW THE BALL HARD ENOUGH THE PINS HIT EACH OTHER, I GUESS THEY *WILL* ALL GET KNOCKED DOWN.
THOUGH IT IS FAIRLY LUCK-BASED.
GUESS THAT'S BETTER THAN TRYING AND FAILING AT PRECISION.

SEEMS HE'S STILL HUNG UP ON YOUR LAST MATCH...
...!!
N-NO WAY, SENPAI ...
WHAT'RE YOU GONNA DO? MAKING HIM MAD WILL JUST INCREASE HIS POWER.

YOU POOR THING!
YOU'RE SUCH A LONER, YOU WENT BOWLING ALONE ?!
SHUT UP!!
GET OFF THAT SUB-JECT!!

...
SUU...
WHY RILE HIM UP MORE?
NOW HE'S GONNA THROW HARD AGAIN.
FRAME 2
?!
YOU CAN DO IT, SENPAI !!
JOLT
ガ SHOCK
THUNK
AHH...
SMRK...
YES...
I WAS JUST CHEERING HIM ON, AFTER ALL...
CLENCH
D-DIRTY ...!

IT'S ALL GOOD.
IF YOU'RE GONNA USE POWER, I'LL JUST RUIN IT WITH UNDER-HANDED-NESS!
SUGOI DEKAI
DON'T SMILE WHEN YOU SAY THAT...
UZAKI WENT ALL-OUT WITH HER DIRTY MOVES...
WHILE MUSCLE-FOR-BRAINS SAKURAI ENDURED.
Hana
Brat
Hottie
20
40
Gorilla Power
AND AT THE END OF THIS MUD-SLINGING MATCH...

WINNER: SAKURAI.
HAAH... HAAH...
IT WAS A PAINFUL BATTLE...
TCH!
MAYBE YOU SHOULD'VE FOCUSED ON YOUR OWN PLAYING, UZAKI.
FOO FOO FOOO...
※Whistle.
IT'S FINE, ITSUHITO.
I'M USED TO IT.
THERE'S SOMETHING FREAKIN' WRONG WITH YOU TWO.
NOW THEN...
YOU SAID WE COULD ORDER WHOEVER LOST TO DO ANYTHING, RIGHT?
I DIDN'T SAY *ANYTHING!*
LEAN
WHISPER
WHISPER
SOMETHING PERVY
NO.
I'LL SAVE IT FOR LATER.
WHAT?! YOU PITIFUL SOUL!
WHY DON'T WE HAVE ANOTHER GAME?
YEAH, SURE.

YOU WANNA GO?
I'LL WIN THIS NEXT ONE AND EARN THE RIGHT TO GIVE ORDERS!
LET'S GO!
YOU FOOL. YOUR ONLY TACTIC'S INTERFERENCE. I'M NOT LETTING YOU BEAT ME.
WHY'RE YOU ONLY THIS AGGRESSIVE WITH EACH OTHER?
JUST FORGET ABOUT THE BET.
STEALING THE PODIUM FROM SENPAI IS MY REASON FOR LIVING!
I WON'T LET THIS END WITH MY LOSS...
I DON'T WANT YOU BEATING ME, UZAKI.
O-OKAY... YOU GUYS DO WHAT YOU WANT.
AND SO SAKAKI REALIZED THAT NONE COULD TRESPASS UPON THE TERRITORY BETWEEN UZAKI AND SAKURAI.
BUT EVEN AS HE THOUGHT, THESE GUYS ARE INCAPABLE OF HAVING FUN LIKE NORMAL PEOPLE, HE ALSO THOUGHT...
JUST MAKE HER DO SOMETHING PERVY.

HAH!
SUGOI

Uzaki-chan Wants to Hang Out!

TODAY IS MY FIRST TIME BOULDERING WITH SENPAI.

HEY SENPAI, LOOK AT THE WALL.

WHOA ...

I SAW THAT IN THE NEWS.

Chapter 29:
The Kouhai and Bouldering

I'VE NEVER TRIED THIS SPORT, SO I'M KIND OF EXCITED.

SKFF

SKFF

WHY BOULDERING, THOUGH?

IT'S UNUSUAL FOR YOU TO SUGGEST SOMETHING TO DO.

HMM...

I GUESS SWIMMING AND BOWLING REMINDED ME OF HOW FUN SPORTS CAN BE.

I WANTED TO DO SOME-THING ATH-LETIC...
BUT I'M NOT GREAT AT BALL SPORTS...
YEAH, THAT WOULD MAKE IT TRICKY...
SINCE MOST OF THE SPORTS YOU CAN JUST START UP ON ARE BALL SPORTS.
WITH BOULDER-ING, YOU CAN MAKE FULL USE OF YOUR MUS-CLES...
WHICH IS GREAT FOR YOU, SINCE YOU'RE TERRIBLE AT CON-TROLLING YOUR STRENGTH.
NICE CHOICE OF WORDS...
LET'S GET THIS PAIR TRYOUT COURSE STARTED!
OKAY!

IN BOULDERING, YOU CLIMB USING HOLDS ATTACHED TO THE WALL.
BUT...
YOU CAN'T JUST CLIMB HOWEVER YOU LIKE!
THERE ARE FIXED ROUTES FOR EVERY LEVEL.
THERE'S COLORED TAPE STUCK NEAR EACH HOLD. YOU CAN ONLY USE HOLDS OF THE SAME COLOR.
REALLY?
SO CLIMBING REQUIRES A LOT OF THINKING, HUH?
YEP!
AN ADVANCED CLIMBER WILL MAKE A CAREFUL PLAN BEFORE STARTING.
THIS IS IMPORTANT!
HM HMM...
SO I CAN'T JUST RELY ON MUSCLE.

IN GENERAL, YOU START AT THE TAPE WITH AN S WRITTEN ON IT AND AIM FOR THE G TAPE.
G
THAT'S ENOUGH BORING EXPLANATIONS FOR NOW. LET'S START CLIMBING!
THERE'S MATS ON THE GROUND, BUT PLEASE BE CAREFUL.
OKAY!
THE START POSITION FOR YOUR HANDS IS MARKED WITH TAPE...
SO MAKE SURE YOU BEGIN YOUR CLIMB WITH THOSE HOLDS.
GREAT!
YEAH!

AND THAT'S IT!
HOW WAS IT?!
TMP
DMP
THAT WAS FUN!
WHEW!
TH--
KOFF!
THAT WAS CRAZY HARD!!
FWAAH
HWEE
WHEEZE
QUITE THE CON-TRAST.
IT TAKES A LOT OF STRENGTH, BUT IT'S REALLY AN INTELLECTU-AL SPORT, HUH?
HAAH!
HAAH!
THERE'S THE CLIMBING ROUTE, THE ORDER YOU SWITCH HAND AND FOOT POSITIONS, THE HOLDS YOU GRIP...
NOD NOD
I didn't... have th'energy... t'think...
WHEEZE
HWEE
HAAH
HWEE
That was... all I could handle...
TREMBLE
MY MUSCLES... IMME-DIATELY HIT... THEIR LIMIT...
NOD NOD
TREMBLE
TREMBLE

THIS SPORT IS KINDA AWFUL, ISN'T IT?
YOU THINK?
I'M HAVING FUN.
WHEEZE
WHEEZE
I'M SURE!
YOU'VE GOT SO MUCH ENERGY, IT'S MAKING ME MAD!
WHEEZE
WHEEZE
WHEEZE
YOU'RE PRETTY OUT OF SHAPE, AREN'T YOU?
SNAP
YOU KNOW IT'S WEIRD TO ENJOY BRUTALIZING YOURSELF, RIGHT?!
HM?
FRUS-TRATED YOU COULDN'T STEAL THE PODIUM FROM ME, HUH?
WHY'RE YOU SO ENER-GETIC?!
NGHHHHH!
I DO WORK OUT IN MY SPARE TIME, YOU KNOW.
WHAT?!
I'M NOT FRUS-TRATED AT ALL!
GOOD FOR YOU FOR BUILDING USELESS MUS-CLES!

YOU'VE STILL GOT LOTS OF ENERGY, HUH?
WHAT?!
LET'S BUMP UP THE DIFFI-CULTY!
GASP! GASP!
THE RULES ARE THE SAME AS BEFORE, BUT THIS WALL'S EVEN HIGHER!
WHOA!
LOOOOM
HOW HIGH IS THIS?
ABOUT EIGHT METERS!
IT LOOKS LIKE... IT'D BE BAD IF WE FELL...
HWEE
IT WOULD BE BAD!
SO YOU'LL BE USING ROPES AND HAR-NESSES FOR THIS NEXT PART!
UM, ARE YOUR LUNGS OKAY?
HWEE
WE CALL THIS SPORT CLIMB-ING!
...
I'LL GO FIRST.
YOU CATCH YOUR BREATH.

I SEE. THE HEIGHT...
MAKES IT EVEN TOUGHER!
OH MAN, I'M KINDA STARTING TO HAVE FUN!
SHWF
HUH? WHERE'S THE FOOTHOLD?
SHWF
AND HOLD ON, I CAN'T SEE DOWN.
SENPAI... OTHER LEG FIRST...
LET ME GIVE THE INSTRUCTIONS-- YOU REST.
IF YOU PUT YOUR RIGHT LEG UP NEXT, THE REST WILL BE EASY!
??
WHERE IS THE HOLD?!
A LITTLE ABOVE YOUR RIGHT KNEE!
I CAN'T TELL! WHERE?!
TREMBLE
TREMBLE
TREMBLE
HE'S HOLDING HIMSELF WITH JUST HIS ARMS!
IS HE REALLY A BEGINNER?!
HE'S LIKE SOME KIND OF BUG...
RIGHT AFTER THIS, SAKURAI GOT TO THE GOAL THE NORMAL WAY.

THAT WAS PRETTY INTERESTING.
WHY ARE YOU SO NONCHALANT ABOUT THIS?
YOU'RE SUCH A MUSCLEHEAD.
HAVE YOU MANAGED TO RECOVER, UZAKI?
MAYBE YOU SHOULD TAKE A BREAK.
NGH... HE'S STRAIGHT UP HAVING FUN, SO EVEN MY TEASING'S NOT WORKING.
MRR!
WHAT?! I'M FINE! I'LL SHOW YOU!!
SNAP
UH, I MEAN, IT LOOKS LIKE YOU'RE STRUGGLING.
WHY'RE YOU SNAPPING AT ME?
FORGET IT. IT'S MORE THAN TWICE AS HIGH AS THE OTHER...
I'M GOIN' UP! AGHHH!!!
UH...

TWO MINUTES LATER, AT THE FOUR-METER POINT...
UZAKI HAS COMPLETELY STOPPED.
I CAN'T ...
YOU LOOK LIKE A COCOON ...
I'LL BE HERE FOREVER...
UNABLE TO ADVANCE OR RETREAT...
STOP SULKING!
I'LL LOWER YOU WITH THE ROPE--JUST RELAX, IT'S OKAY!
THAT WAS A BIT MUCH, HUH?
TAKE A LITTLE BREAK. IF YOU FEEL LIKE YOU WANT TO GO AGAIN, JUST CALL FOR ME.
HAAH!
THANK YOU...
HAAH!
HAAH!
HAAH!
I THINK THAT'S ALL SHE'S GOT FOR TODAY...

YOU'VE STILL GOT TIME LEFT-- WHAT WOULD YOU LIKE TO DO?
YOU'RE FREE TO USE THE REST OF THE FACILITY.
HMM...
UZAKI, DO YOU WANNA LEAVE?
YOU CAN CLIMB, SENPAI.
I'M NOT READY TO MOVE YET, SO I'LL JUST WATCH.
BUT...
YOU'RE HAVING FUN, RIGHT?
NOW THAT YOU'VE FINALLY GOT THE CHANCE TO DO SOME-THING SERIOUSLY ATHLETIC.
I DIDN'T THINK YOU'D CHOOSE A CONTEST WHERE YOU'D HAVE A TOTAL ADVAN-TAGE OVER ME.
YOU GOT ME.
IF YOU FEEL BAD, JUST TREAT ME TO DINNER TONIGHT.
WHAT A DIRTY TRAP, SENPAI. I RAISE THE WHITE FLAG OF SURREN-DER-- *THIS* TIME.
YOU BRAT...

SEEING YOU LIKE THAT IS LIKE BEING BACK IN HIGH SCHOOL, SENPAI...
HEH HEH...
SAKU-RAI-SENPAI.

THE USUAL.

Uzaki-chan Wants to Hang Out!

IT HAPPENED VERY SUDDENLY.
BA-KRK
...!!!

Chapter 30:
The Kouhai and Reminiscing

BOSS?!
WHAT HAP-PENED?!
QUIV
AH, YOU STRAINED YOUR BACK.
IT'S BEEN A WHILE SINCE THE LAST TIME.
QUIV
E...
EMER-GENCY CLO-SURE TODAY...
QUIV
I'M CLOSING UP SHOP TO GO TO THE CHIRO...
QUIV
QUIV
EFFEC-TIVE IMMEDI-ATELY...
HMM... GUESS WE HAVE NO CHOICE.

ANYONE HAVE A DRIVER'S LICENSE?
ME.
FWUP
テキ
SHWF
パキ
SHWF
CAN YOU TAKE DAD TO THE CHIRO-PRACTOR IN OUR CAR, THEN?
HANA-CHAN CAN CLOSE THE CAFÉ WITH ME.
ON IT!
HEL-LO...
SHWF
パキ
SHWF
テキ

I JUST CALLED. THEY SAID THEY CAN TREAT YOU RIGHT AWAY.
GIVE ME YOUR SHOUL-DER, BOSS.
AH, OW... SORRY...

SORRY, IF YOU TWO CAN HANDLE THINGS HERE...
IT'LL BE FINE. LEAVE IT TO US!
TAKE CARE.

I COULD MANAGE THE SHOP FOR THE DAY IF YOU LIKE, THOUGH.
にこぉおおお
SMIIILE
I FEEL LIKE YOU'D HAVE TAKEN IT OVER BY THE TIME I GOT BACK, SO JUST CLOSE UP...

I'M DONE CLEANING.
GREAT, THANKS!
IT FEELS KIND OF STRANGE TO CLOSE WHEN IT'S STILL LIGHT OUT.
CAN I RELAX UNTIL YOU'RE DONE CLOSING THE REGISTER, AMI-SAN?
SURE!
YOU CAN HAVE COFFEE IF YOU LIKE, TOO.
YAY!
I THINK I WILL!
ARE YOU GONNA INHERIT THIS PLACE, AMI-SAN?
Changed clothes.
WELL, I'D LIKE TO INHERIT IT.
OR RATHER...
CON-QUER IT?
THAT'S... AN UNSET-TLING SYN-ONYM...

BUT IT'S NOT SOMETHING I CAN DO RIGHT AFTER GRADUATING.
I'M STILL LACKING MANY OF THE THINGS I NEED.
A DRIVER'S LICENSE, FOR ONE.
GOOD THING SAKURAI-KUN WAS HERE TODAY.
FOR SUCH A GRUMPY GUY, HE'S ALWAYS ANNOYINGLY HELPFUL.
SO PLEASE, USE HIM ALL YOU WANT.
DON'T TALK ABOUT HIM LIKE HE'S A THING...
SO, HE'S ALWAYS BEEN LIKE THAT, HUH?
WHAT WAS HE LIKE IN HIGH SCHOOL?
I HEARD YOU WERE BOTH IN THE SWIM CLUB.

DID YOU TEASE HIM LIKE YOU DO NOW?
AHH...
ACTUALLY, WE ONLY STARTED HANGING OUT IN UNIVER-SITY.
IN HIGH SCHOOL, WE ONLY SAW EACH OTHER AT THE CLUB.
HMM...
SO YOU MET THERE?
UMM, I THINK...
Swim club?
I'm not really good at swim-ming, though.
Uzaki Hana (15)
high school 1st year

No, no--they need managers.

You're not in any clubs anyway, right?

Why don't we do it together?

WHAAAT?

TUG TUG

WAH!

There's this cute third-year guy who went to my junior high.

Please! I'd feel so lonely by myself!

What'll you do once he retires from the club?
SO PUSHY...

Umm...
today we've got two girls joining as managers.
Be nice to them, guys.

おおおおお
YEAAAAH!
YAH!
DON'T CELEBRATE THIS! YOU GUYS ARE PATHETIC!
IT'LL BE TOUGH, SINCE WE'RE A BIG GROUP, SO PLEASE DO YOUR BEST!
YAAAY!♡
Okay, third-year manager-- you handle the rest.
Teach the first-years about the job.
All right, time for warm-ups!!
NICE TO MEET YOU!
Thanks for having us!
Hrmm...

I came because she wanted me to...
but this looks like a serious sports club. I feel really out of place.
Maybe I was a little hasty...
I wonder if this'll work out...
Hey!
Sorry, I'm late 'cause of cleaning duty.
Oh, Saku-rai-kun.
We've got more first-year managers today, so say hi.
Oh...
really?

Hi...
I'm Sakurai, a second-year...
GLARE
Sakurai Shinichi (16)
high school 2nd year

'KAY...
...
Of course, he's not trying to glare at her.

All right, I'm gonna do warm-ups.
?
DO YOUR BEST!

HUH...?
TH...

THAT WAS SCARY!!
He was giving me the stink eye!
There's guys like that here?!
She gets her cowardice from her mother.
It's my first day, and I already want to quit!!
HANA?
Scary...!!
AND, WELL...
HE MADE A BAD FIRST IMPRESSION...
HUNH...
HE DIDN'T ON ME, THOUGH...
......
STILL...

HE'S REALLY EAR-NEST-- SO EVEN THOUGH IT TOOK ME A WHILE TO GET USED TO HIM...
I FOUND OUT PRETTY QUICKLY HE'S NOT SCARY.
AND YOU GOT CLOSER TO HIM AFTER THAT, HUH?
ONE COULD SAY HE'S YOUR ONE AND ONLY.
HUH?
WHAT D'Y'MEAN, "HUH"?
IT'S NOT LIKE YOU CALL ME "SENPAI," OR MY DAD...
HUH?
YOU JUST TALK THAT WAY WHEN SAKURAI-KUN'S AROUND, DON'T YOU?

SEN-PAI! ENOUGH REMI-NISC-ING... I-I'M GOING HOME NOW!
AHH!
SORRY! UM!
I SHOULDN'T HAVE MENTIONED THAT, SHOULD I?!
WERE YOU NOT AWARE YOU WERE DOING THAT?!
SEE YOU LATER...
NO WAY...
SENPAI!
HAVE I DUG UP A LAND-MINE?!!
NO... THIS IS THE GREAT-EST TREA-SURE!
SHIVER...
I'LL MAKE HER TALK ABOUT IT SOME-DAY!!

STILL
GROWING...
BUT
NOT
IN
HEIGHT.

Uzaki-chan Wants to Hang Out!

HAAH!
HAAH!
NLRCH
NLRCH
NLRCH
NLRCH
HAAH!
HAAH!
NLRCH
ぎしっ
NLRCH
SENPAI... HARDER...
NLRCH
NLRCH
HNN...
KNEAD
YEAH... THAT'S GOOD, SAKURAI-KUN!
NLRCH

NLRCH
MAN... KNEADING UDON DOUGH IS HARD, HUH?
NLRCH NLRCH NLRCH
YEAH!
NLRCH
KNEAD ぎゅっ
KNEAD ぎゅっ
ぎゅっし NLRCH
THUNK ばんっ
KNEAD ぎゅっ
THWUMP ばたんっ

Chapter 31:
The Kouhai and Cooking Practice

TODAY, SAKURAI-KUN HAS COME OVER TO LEARN TO COOK.

BE-CAUSE YESTER-DAY...
SMOLDER... ブス...
TNK... コト...
Szzz...
SMOLDER... ブス...
SMOLDER... ブス...

It's Napolitan spaghetti ...
Errr...
PWUFF プス
PWUFF プス
PWUFF プス
This is awful.
Napolitan...? Did you add squid ink or something?
We were gonna expand your duties to cooking soon, but...
BLUSH
URK...
The fork can't even penetrate it.
TINK カッ
KA-TINK カチッ
You live on your own. I thought you'd be able to do a *little* cooking.
I'm sorry... please just laugh at me...
IT WAS SO BAD, THEY COULDN'T EVEN LET HIM DOWN GENTLY.

AHA HA HA HA HA HA!
AHA HA HA HA!
HA HA HA HA HA!
サッ SHWP
サッ SHWP
AHH HA HA!
HA HA HA HA HA!
That's too much laughing.
Y-you're the one who told me to laugh...
ぎり GRNN
ぎり GRNN
ぎり GRNN
LET GOOO...
Agh, no fighting!
All right!
バッ SHWAP

You can't cook! Learn how! Now!
CHOMP
KRNCH
GRRK
Thish ish inedible!
So don't eat it!
Okay, I won't!
You'll practice at my house tomorrow!!
Whaaaaa?!
IT SEEMS THAT WAS HOW IT WENT.
You can practice here, but...
You didn't bother to ask your mom?
Sorry to come on short notice.
You hardly have any cooking tools at your place, Senpai.
Mom's my cooking teacher!
Learn from the best!
BOW
Please teach me, ma'am.
BA-DMP

MOM POWER!
LEAVE IT TO MOM!
FWUP

ALL THESE COMPLI-MENTS GOT "MOM" FEEL-ING RATHER GOOD ABOUT HERSELF-- UNBECOM-INGLY SO FOR A FORTY-THREE-YEAR-OLD.

AND NOW HERE WE ARE...
WHEW——— ...
I'M GLAD YOU'RE TEACH-ING ME, BUT...

JUST GOING STRAIGHT TO UDON NOO-DLES?

WOULDN'T IT BE BETTER TO START WITH SOME-THING EASIER?

YES, YES-- LOOKING GOOD.

BUT SAKU-RAI-KUN...

UDON IS SUR-PRISINGLY SIMPLE.

THE ONLY INGREDI-ENTS ARE FLOUR, SALT, AND WATER.

THOUGH THE BROTH IS ANOTHER THING.

WAIT, THAT'S IT?!

IS THAT RIGHT?

IT MIGHT SEEM DIFFICULT TO MAKE UDON, BUT ACTUALLY, IT'S HARD FOR EVEN BEGINNERS TO SCREW UP! IT TAKES TIME, SO TRY IT OUT ON THE WEEKEND!

(1) Dissolve salt in lukewarm water and gradually mix in the flour.

(2) Knead it hard into dough.

(3) Once the dough has formed, take it out of the bowl, then continue to stretch and fold the dough. Doing this will improve the texture!

THERE'S NO MORE SPACE HERE, SO GOOGLE THE REST! *MEOW!*

KNEADING IS HARD WORK! IT TAKES SOME STRENGTH.
BUT BOYS *DO* HAVE MUSCLE!
THAT'S SENPAI'S ONE REDEEMING FEATURE. HE EVEN HAS MUSCLES FOR BRAINS!
HANA!
IT'S FINE. SHE'S ALWAYS LIKE THAT.

SOME-HOW...
WE'VE BEEN HAVING A NORMAL CONVER-SATION...
ALWAYS?
WELL... YES...
I'M SORRY SHE HAS SUCH A SHARP TONGUE...
WHY WOULD...
BOOOO
OH!
HE'S ONLY LOOKING AT THE UDON, SO THERE'S NO SCARY GLAR-ING!
AS LONG AS HE ISN'T GLARING, HE'S POLITE AND ACTUALLY PRETTY EASY TO TALK TO!!
I'VE DISCOVERED AN ATTACK STRATEGY!!
UZAKI-CHAN'S MOM IS ALSO RUDE BY NATURE-- SHE JUST KEEPS MORE OF HER THOUGHTS TO HERSELF.

MY APOLOGIES FOR ALL THAT, SAKURAI-KUN.
?
NO, IT'S FINE.
HUNH...
(4) If it's hard to knead with your arms, put it in a clean plastic bag and stomp your heels on it. Just make sure the bag doesn't rip!
WE'LL LEAVE IT TO SIT ABOUT TWENTY MINUTES. YOU TWO TAKE A BREAK.
THE YOUNG-STERS SHOULD BE ALONE TO-GETHER.
I'LL GO DO THE LAUNDRY...
OHO HO HO!
OKAY!
SENPAI, WANNA DRINK?
YOU WORKED UP A BIT OF A SWEAT, RIGHT?
YEAH, SOME TEA...
CATS ...!!
GULP...

PHEW...
I FELT UNEASY AT FIRST, BUT I WAS ABLE TO CHAT A LOT WITH SAKURAI-KUN.
POOP CAT
HE'S DILIGENT AND GOOD, JUST LIKE THE PEOPLE AT HIS JOB SAY, ISN'T HE?
YEAH!
AND NOW I KNOW I'M FINE WITH HIM, TOO.
AS LONG AS I DON'T LOOK HIM-IN-THE EYE!
AND WANTING TO LEARN TO COOK EVEN THOUGH HE'S A BOY...
HOW MODERN!
HE'S THE SORT WHO MIGHT MAKE A GOOD HUSBAND.
HEH HEH...
IT'S FINE, SENPAI. YOU CAN DO IT.

YOU SAID YOU WANNA TOUCH 'EM TODAY FOR SURE, RIGHT?
※ She means the cats.
I'd like to touch that pussy someday.
TOUCH THEM ?!
※ Has the wrong idea.
OH, BUT SHE'S STILL SO WARY...
I'D FEEL BAD IF I SCARED HER...
THAT'S NOT WHAT I...
I AM SCARED! I AM, BUT...!
SHE WAS GLANCING AT YOU-- THAT MEANS SHE'S INTERESTED.
STAAARE
FIDGET
FIDGET
AND SIT DOWN ALREADY.
I...
I WAS LOOKING, BUT NOT LIKE THAT!
YOU SHOULD JUST GO RIGHT FOR IT! HARD!
HANA ?!
NO, SHE'LL BOLT IF I DO THAT...
SAKURAI-KUN?!

THIS IS NO GOOD! I THOUGHT THINGS HAD GOTTEN EASIER BETWEEN US, BUT I JUST DON'T UNDERSTAND THAT BOY...
AND WHY IS HANA TRYING SO HARD TO OFFER UP HER OWN MOTHER?!
※She's not.

NO, I CAN'T. I CAN'T GIVE UP.

SLIDE...

IT'S NOT TOO LATE!

SORRY TO MAKE YOU WAIT...

I MUST COR-RECT... THE ERROR OF THEIR WAYS!

SHALL WE... BOIL THE UDON?

THAT'S MY JOB, AS AN ADULT!!
IN THE SUMMER OF UZAKI TSUKI'S FORTY-THIRD YEAR...
A SENSE OF PURPOSE AWOKE WITHIN HER.
RIGHT?
HAND-MADE NOODLES ARE GREAT!
STAAAARE
SHWRL
SHWRL
SHWRL
HUNH

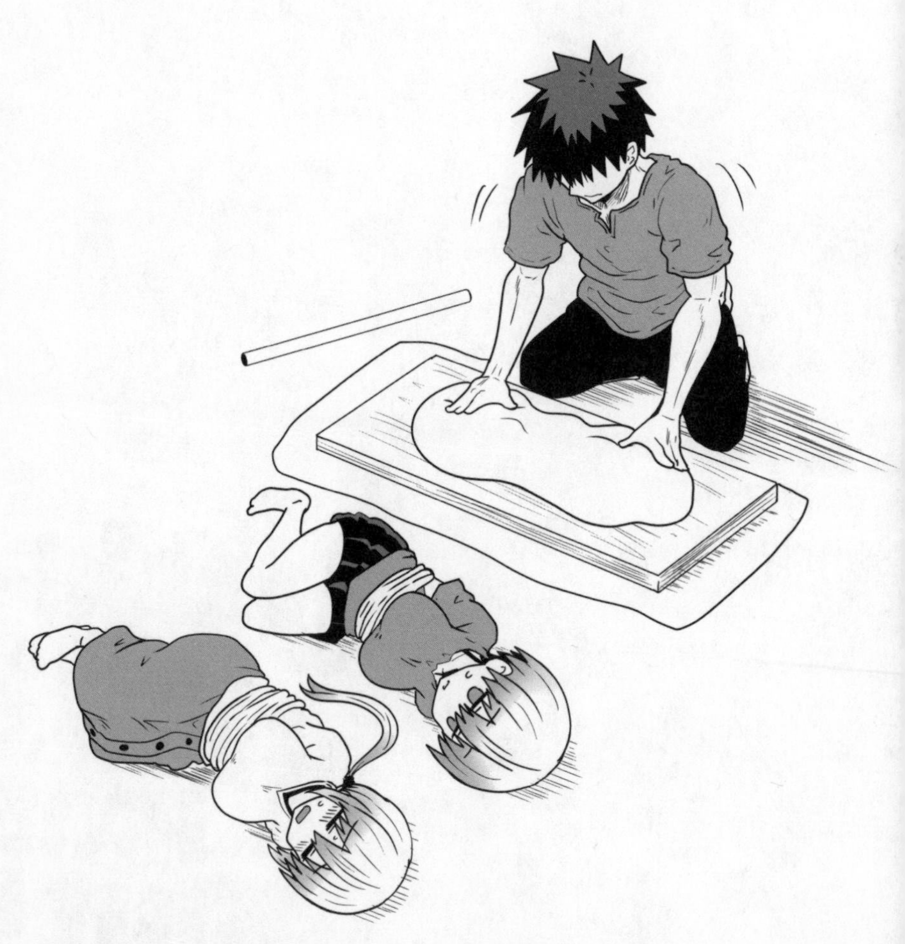

Uzaki-chan Wants to Hang Out!

25
RAY
SUU...

IT FEELS LIKE THAT GOOD-BYE WAS EVEN LONGER AGO... ♫
MY HEELS ARE WORN, I'VE SEALED AWAY THAT HEART-BREAKING GLOW... ♫

WHEN I HAD YOU I BARELY SAW THAT COMET'S RAIN-BOW... ♫

BUT NOW I CAN'T ANY-MORE. NOW I CAN'T ANY-MORE... ♫
THOUGH IT'S ALL I'M LOOKING FOR. ♫

WE WERE ALWAYS SING-ING... ♫
IN THE MOMENT AND I... ♫

NEVER FELT SO LONELY... ♫
AS I DID WHEN THE SKY... ♫

Chapter 32: The Kouhai, Karaoke, and Cosplay

YOU DIDN'T HAFTA SHTOP INNA MIDDLE!
SHORRY FOR BOTHER-IN' YOU!
YOU'RE A PRETTY GOOD SHINGER, SHENPAI!
SNERK
SNERK
DON'T COWER INNA CORNER LIKE THAT! WE'RE SHORRY!
STAAARE
YOU'RE LOOKIN' AT USH LIKE A SHTRAY CAT THAT DOESHN'T TRUSHT HUMANSH, SHENPAI.
TOOK HIS SHOES OFF, AS IS PROPER.

BUT, WELL...
SMIRK
SMIRK
I WASHN'T REALLY SHURPRISHED. YOU ARE THE GUY WHO GOESH TO THE MOVIESH ALONE.
I KNEW IT! YOU DO SHOLO KARAOKE, TOO!
ORDER ME A BEER, TOO!
WE WERE INNA AREA DRINKIN', AND WE JUSHT HAPPENED TO SHEE YOU, SHAKURAI-KUN.
THEY'VE BOTH DRUNK A LOT...
PARDON ME, THIS IS ROOM TWENTY-FIVE...
PLEASE ADD TWO PEOPLE.
I'LL PAY AFTER...
FROM NOW ON, I'M USING A DIFFERENT KARAOKE PARLOR.
SOLO KARAOKE!!
ITS MAIN PURPOSE IS TO PRACTICE SINGING AND VOCALIZATION...
AND TO LET OFF STRESS.
THEY SAY THIS KIND OF PRACTICE IS EFFECTIVE AND KEEPS YOU FROM FUMBLING LYRICS AT IMPORTANT GATHERINGS...
SO SOLO KARAOKE IS ON THE RISE.

HOW-EVER!!

THE GENERAL VIEW OF KARAOKE AS A SOCIAL ACTIVITY IS STILL QUITE DEEP-ROOTED...

SO IF ACQUAIN-TANCES SPOT YOU, ODDS ARE HIGH THEY'LL TEASE YOU.

AND EVEN THE FRONT DESK...

A LONER, HUH?

MAY SECRETLY JUDGE YOU.

BUT THAT'S NOTHING COMPARED TO THE SHAME OF MAKING MISTAKES IN THE RAP SECTIONS...

OR SINGING POORLY IN FRONT OF FRIENDS OR LOVERS.

RISING TO THE CHALLENGE OF SOLO KARAOKE...

REQUIRES A PROUDLY INDE-PENDENT SPIRIT!

RAWR!!

DROOP

HEEEY, SHEN-PAAAI,

DON'T BE MAD! SHEN-PAAAI!

YOU STUPID DRUNK...

CACKLE

CACKLE CACKLE

ANYWAY, UZAKI, AMI-SAN...
HAAAH———...
THOUGH WE MAY WORK AND ATTEND SCHOOL TOGETHER, YOU HAVE TO RE-SPECT PRIVACY...
HWEE——!!
SHA
SHAKA SHA SHA
ENOUGH WITH THE MA-RACAS!!
SHAKA
SHA
SHAKA
SHAKA
SHAKA

GULP
HANA-SHAN...
MAYBE YA SHOULD SHOW SHAKURAI-KUN SHOME-THIN', TO APOLO-GIZE?
MUR MUR
HUH?
MUR MUR

SHAKU-RAI-KUN, WE'RE GOIN' T' THE BATHROOM FOR A BIT.
OKAY...

SHORRY FOR THE WAIT!

TA-DAA!
UH. WHAT'S THAT?
EH HEH HEH.
THISH IS A BIT EMBARRASSHING.
THEY LEND OUT COSHPLAY AT T' FRONT DESHK. WE TRIED SHOME ON!
WHY ...?
NEVER MIND WHY~!
ANYWAY, DRINK!
ぎゅむ
MUSH

?!
ぎゅう
SQUISH
ぎゅう
SQUISH
SCOOT SCOOT...

WH...
WHY'RE YOU ON EITHER SIDE...?
WELL...
JUSH DOIN' A LIL' SHOME-THIN' SHOME-THIN' FOR YOU.

WE DID INTER-RUPT YOUR KARAOKE, AND SHO IT'S LIKE, SHOR-RRRY, RIGHT?
TAKING ADVANTAGE.
......
PET
PET
EH HEH HEH... LOOKIT THESHE ARMSH...
YOU'RE CLINGING A LIL' HARD, AMI-SHAN.
MGH!
MWOMP
.....!!

SHOOO? FEELING BET-TER~?
UH... I MEAN... I'M JUST CON-FUSED...
PROD
PROD
YA DON'T LIKE IT?
STEAM
STEAM
IT'S NOT ABOUT LIKING IT OR NOT LIKING IT OR LICKING... UH...
PLEASE, NO MORE OF THIS.
Sakurai is bewildered!
OKAY!
HANA-CHAN, NEXT COS-TUME!
HE'S A STUB-BORN ONE!!
HUF
HOW D'YOU LIKE THIS ?!!

THOSE GETUPS ARE REALLY OUT THERE, TOO...
UH... I MEAN, I CAN'T REALLY...
AMI-SHAN, AMI-SHAN, AMI-SHAN...
THISH COSH-TUME IS A LIL' MUCH...
OOH LA LA! ♡ (SFX)
IT'S FINE, IT'S FINE!
IT COV-ERSH MORE THAN A SHWIM-SHUIT!
SHO, SHA-KURAI-KUN?!
NOT GRUMPY ANY-MORE, RIGHT?
BA-SHK
UH, THIS IS BEYOND THAT...
I FEEL LIKE THIS ISN'T A PLACE A NORMAL PERSON SHOULD BE IN...
DID AMI-SAN JUST WANT TO MAKE UZAKI WEAR THAT?
YOU'RE SHO CALM!!
I MEAN, I *AM* THE SOBER ONE HERE.

I'M TIRED...
I GIVE IN...
YEAH, YEAH. I'M NOT MAD ANYMORE.
HAAH...
LET'S ALL JUST ENJOY SOME KARAOKE.
YAY!
I FEEL LIKE COMPLAINING WILL JUST ESCALATE THIS...
I'LL JUST BE LIKE "YEAH, YEAH" TO GET THROUGH THIS...
MEH HEH! THASH WHAT I LIKE ABOUT YOU, SHAKURAI-KUN.
YEAH, YEAH, THANKS.
SHO CAN I DO A SHONG?
YEAH, YEAH, GO AHEAD.
CAN I GET MORE BOOZE?
YEAH, YEAH, JUST DON'T DRINK TOO MUCH.
DIDJA HAVE A FAVORITE COSHPLAY?
YEAH, YEAH, I LIKED THE BUNNY GIRL.
PWAH—
I CAN'T BEAT DRUNKS.
AH!!
AH...
AH...

OH... MAN...
DIDN'T THINK YOU'D ANSHWER THAT...
PER-VERT...
WAIT, NO! I JUST ...!
......
DON'T WORRY ABOUT IT!
ALL MEN LOVE BUNNY GIRLS!
あっはっはっ
AHA HA
はっ
HA!
MAYBE I'LL DRINK SOME BOOZE, TOO...
HAAAH
It's always wise to avoid drunks.

YOU A PERVERT OR WHAT?

Uzaki-chan Wants to Hang Out!

WHAT'S SENPAI LIKE WHEN HE'S DRUNK?

Chapter 33:
The Kouhai and Bad Booze

I DON'T THINK I'VE EVER SEEN HIM DRUNK.
GOOD POINT...
NOW THAT YOU MENTION IT.

DOES HE CRY, LAUGH, GET MAD, PICK FIGHTS ...?
I CAN'T REALLY IMAGINE IT.
MAYBE HE JUST DOESN'T GET DRUNK 'CAUSE HE CAN HOLD HIS LIQUOR?
STAARE

THEY SAY MOST PEOPLE GET LESS INHIBITED. BUT I WONDER HOW IT IS WITH SAKURAI-KUN...
HRM...
PERSON-ALLY, I HOPE HE HAS A TENDENCY TO STRIP OR SOME-THING.
YOU'D LIKE THAT, WOULDN'T YOU, AMI-SAN?
THAT REALLY IS PER-SONAL...

OH, SAKU DOES GET DRUNK.
SLUUURP
HE JUST KNOWS HIS LIMITS AND RESPECTS 'EM.
I THINK HE CAN HOLD HIS BOOZE PRETTY WELL, THOUGH.
OH, I SEE.
CLAP

AS ONE OF HIS FEW FRIENDS, YOU'VE SEEN HIM DRUNK--RIGHT, SAKAKI-SAN?
DON'T SAY "FEW FRIENDS."
BUT YEAH.
AT CLASS PARTIES AND STUFF.

WHAT WAS HE LIKE?
HOW MUCH DOES HE HAVE TO DRINK?
WHY? YOU WANNA GET HIM DRUNK AND ATTACK HIM?
HM?

NO...IT'S JUST KIND OF IRRITATING I'M THE ONLY ONE EMBARRASSING MYSELF, OVER AND OVER...
I'D LIKE TO DRAG HIM DOWN WITH ME...
I HAVE TO PLOT SOMETHING FOR WHEN HE HAS A DAY OFF.
PRETTY SURE YOU BRING THAT ON YOURSELF.
YOU'RE AN ADULT. DRINK RESPONSIBLY.

BUT IF YOU WANT TO GET HIM DRUNK...
I GUESS I COULD TELL YOU.
YES!
THANK YOU SO MUCH!
GUESS WE NEED TO SET UP A PARTY.
WHEN SHOULD WE DO IT?

AFTER LAST TIME, AMI-SAN...
I'D LIKE TO HANDLE THIS ON MY OWN.
OH NO! ARE YOU MAD, HANA-CHAN?!

THAT NIGHT...
DING DOONG

HEY, YOU'RE HERE.
KA-CHAK ガチャ

THIS IS SUDDEN, COMING OVER TO DRINK AT HOME. WHAT'S UP?
OHHH, NOTH-ING!
ACT NATURAL! NATURAL!
WE DON'T HAVE MUCH SUMMER VACA-TION LEFT...
I FIGURED THIS WAS THE ONLY TIME WE COULD.
RUSTLE...
ガサ...
WELL, IF YOU'RE MAKING DINNER FOR ME, I'M HAPPY...
I BOUGHT A BUNCH OF DIF-FERENT DRINKS.
RUMMAGE
RUMMAGE
"SAKU DOESN'T DRINK MUCH WHEN HE'S OUT...
"BE-CAUSE IT MAKES GET-TING HOME A PAIN.
"BUT IF YOU'RE DRINKING AT HOME, WHERE HE DOESN'T HAVE TO WORRY ABOUT ANY OF THAT, HE LETS HIS GUARD DOWN A BIT!
FIRST STAGE: CLEAR!
OKAY THEN, I'LL GET COOK-ING!

WOW!
THANK YOU!
YOU REALLY ARE A GREAT COOK!
EH HEH HEH!
YOU SHOULD COME OVER TO PRACTICE AGAIN.
STEAM
SO YOU CAN ACTUALLY MAKE CHILI SHRIMP AT HOME?
STEAM
YOU'RE BASI-CALLY A PRO.
THAT'S AN EXAGGER-ATION, REALLY.
EEE HEE HEE!
"MAKE THE FOOD SPICY AND FLAVORFUL TO KEEP HIM DRINKING.
WHY DON'T WE WATCH A MOVIE OR SOME-THING?
SOUNDS GOOD.
THERE'S ACTUALLY THIS NEW SHOW I WANTED TO SEE.
"IT'S EVEN BETTER IF YOU CAN DISTRACT HIM FROM HIS GLASS...
"TO KEEP HIM FROM THINKING ABOUT HOW MUCH HE'S DRINKING.
SECOND AND THIRD STAGES: CLEAR!

"AFTER THAT, JUST GET HIM TO DRINK LOTS.
GULP グイ
"HE'S COMPETITIVE AND GOES WITH THE FLOW,
"SO IF OTHERS ARE DRINKING, HE'LL KEEP DRINKING, TOO."
グイ GULP
THERE'S NO POINT IF I'M DRUNK, SO I'LL JUST PRETEND!
IT'S A CAN, SO HE CAN'T SEE INSIDE!
HEY, SENPAI-- HERE, HERE!
GLUP
GLUP
HMM? AH, SORRY.
THANKS.
GRIN
GRIN
OH, IT'S NOTHING~!
GRIN
GRIN
HERE, HAVE SOME MORE.
DRINK UP, DRINK UP!
FOUR HOURS LATER...
グデ DEAD
WHEW...
HE'S FINALLY GETTING WHERE I WANT HIM...

BUT THIS IS WHERE IT REALLY STARTS, SENPAI!!
EHEE HEE
HEE HEE HEE
"SAKURAI BECOMES USELESS WHEN HE DRINKS!"
Use-less...? How, specifi-cally?
※Drink responsibly, and don't force others to drink!
He can talk and respond, but his judgment gets dubious.
And he looks pretty ridicu-lous, too.
Oho.
That does sound use-less!
You sound glad.
When he's drunk, he can't think and talk at the same time.
He can't lie or hide things, either. His de-fenses are down.
He doesn't want to get like that in front of people, so he's learned to hold back.
I see...

YOU LOOK LIKE YOU'RE REALLY ENJOYING YOURSELF--HUH, SENPAI?

URK... CUT IT OUT...
YOU'RE SO DEFENSELESS! THIS'D USUALLY BE UNTHINKABLE!
AHA HA HA!
POKE
POKE
HEH HEH HEH!

HEY... THANSH... FER ALWAYSH COOKIN' FER ME...

YOU'RE HONEST WHEN YOU'RE DRUNK--HUH, SENPAI?

YOU'RE ALWAYS HOLDING BACK, THEN?
YEAH ...
BLINK
BLINK
INTERESTING!
YOU'LL ANSWER HONESTLY TO EVERYTHING!

I'D BE EVEN HAPPIER IF YOU'D SAY STUFF LIKE THAT WITHOUT BOOZE.
IT'S EMBARRASSHING... SHO I CAN'T...

ANYTHIN
ELSE
YOU
CAN'T
USUALL
SAY?
DROOP
DROOP
HNN
...
I
LIKE
YOU...
R...
カクッ
SLUMP
COOK-
ING...
......
グイ
GULP

ブッ
BWAH!
TNK
カン
SST

GULP
GULP
GULP

ゴッ
GLUG
ゴブ
GLUG
GLUG
ゴブ

グビ
GLUG
グビ
GLUG
TNK
SST
グビ
GLUG

PARDON ME.
GOOD THING I TOLD UZAKI TO LEAVE THE DOOR UN-LOCKED.
I JUST CAME TO CHECK ON THINGS, BUT...

パタム
TUNK

SNRRR
SNRRR
I WAS EXPECTING SAKU-- BUT WHY IS UZAKI DRUNK?
SHE'S GONNA HAVE TO STAY OVER NOW.
HNNN...
HNN...
HNN...
HEY, SAKU-- YOU OKAY?
AH!
HUH? ITSHU-HITO...? WHA...?
DON'T WORRY ABOUT IT. I'LL LAY DOWN A FUTON, SO SLEEP HERE.
YOU SHOULD TOO, UZAKI.
AGH...
URGH...
I'LL LOCK UP. DON'T WORRY, JUST GO TO BED.
SNUG
SNUG
AH... THANKS...
SEE YOU.
CHK
SWEET DREAMS...

うと NOD...
THERE'S SOME-THING...
NOD... うと...
?

? ?
SOME-THING'S WEIRD...
SU——...

AFTER THAT, THEY PASSED RIGHT OUT.
ガク SLUMP...
WHAT IS IT...?
SNRR... スヤ...

Extra: The Kouhai and Cooking Practice

MOM, TRY THIS.

THIS KIN-PIRA...

WHAT DO YOU THINK?

YOU DID WELL!

YAY!

WHAT SHOULD I MAKE NEXT?

YOU USUALLY MAKE DISHES WITH MEAT...
BUT LATELY, YOU'VE BEEN DOING VEGETA-BLES.
SZZZ
I WANTED TO INCREASE MY SIDE DISH REP-ERTOIRE.
LATELY HANA'S BEEN COMING TO ME WANTING TO LEARN TO COOK THINGS.
SZZZ

HUH? YOU'RE MAKING STUFF AGAIN?
WANT ME TO TASTE TEST IT FOR YOU?
Little brother Kiri, high school second-year.
SURE, I GUESS.
NOT TOO MUCH. IT'S FOR DINNER.
I KNEW IT. SO THAT'S WHY SHE'S DOING IT.
IT'S FUN TO TEACH HANA-- SHE LEARNS SO QUICKLY...
ONCE IT CHANGES COLOR, TAKE IT OUT RIGHT AWAY WITH THE STRAINER.
IF YOU OVERBOIL IT, THE TEXTURE GETS RUINED.
ザァァァァ
SHAAAAA
HOW ABOUT THIS?
TRY THIS!
MOM!
BUT WHEN EVERY DAY IS LIKE THIS...

PHEW...
PLSH!!
HAAH——...
SHE'S RATHER CHARMING AND SWEET, IF I DO SAY SO MYSELF...
PLSH...
ちゃぽ...
I HOPE IT PAYS OFF FOR HER...

To be continued...

And so, Volume 3 comes to an end.
I worked really, really hard on this book.
I even tried bouldering in the name of research! (That was hard, too.)

I hope you'll stay with me for Volume 4.
Take care!

Thanks to Terukazu Yoshira-san for help with the Chapter 31 content, and to Ayu Kirishima-san for help with the finishing touches on Chapter 33.

Thank you both very much!

SEVEN SEAS ENTERTAINMENT PRESENTS

Uzaki-chan Wants to Hang Out!

VOLUME 3

story and art by TAKE

TRANSLATION
Jennifer Ward

ADAPTATION
T Campbell

LETTERING
Ludwig Sacramento

COVER DESIGN
KC Fabellon

PROOFREADER
Kurestin Armada

EDITOR
Jenn Grunigen

PREPRESS TECHNICIAN
Rhiannon Rasmussen-Silverstein

PRODUCTION MANAGER
Lissa Pattillo

MANAGING EDITOR
Julie Davis

ASSOCIATE PUBLISHER
Adam Arnold

PUBLISHER
Jason DeAngelis

Seven Seas press and purchase enquiries can be sent to Marketing Manager Lianne Sentar at press@gomanga.com. Information regarding the distribution and purchase of digital editions is available from Digital Manager CK Russell at digital@gomanga.com.

ISBN: 978-1-64505-484-9

Printed in Canada

First Printing: June 2020

10 9 8 7 6 5 4 3 2 1

FOLLOW US ONLINE: www.sevenseasentertainment.com

READING DIRECTIONS

This book reads from ***right to left***, Japanese style. If this is your first time reading manga, you start reading from the top right panel on each page and take it from there. If you get lost, just follow the numbered diagram here. It may seem backwards at first, but you'll get the hang of it! Have fun!!

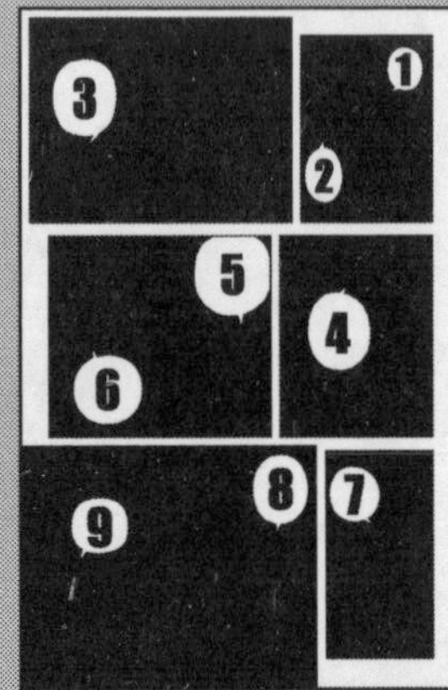